HAL•LEONARD
INSTRUMENTAL PLAY-ALONG

AUDIO ACCESS INCLUDED

PLAYBACK+
Speed • Pitch • Balance • Loop

TRUMPET

Movie and TV Music

Audio Arrangements by Peter Deneff

To access audio visit:
www.halleonard.com/mylibrary

Enter Code
4112-5283-2725-4929

ISBN 978-1-5400-2066-6

D0584799

HAL•LEONARD®

For all works contained herein:
Unauthorized copying, arranging, adapting, recording, Internet posting, public performance,
or other distribution of the music in this publication is an infringement of copyright.
Infringers are liable under the law.

Visit Hal Leonard Online at
www.halleonard.com

Contact Us:
Hal Leonard
7777 West Bluemound Road
Milwaukee, WI 53213
Email: info@halleonard.com

In Europe contact:
Hal Leonard Europe Limited
Distribution Centre, Newmarket Road
Bury St Edmunds, Suffolk, IP33 3YB
Email: info@halleonardeurope.com

In Australia contact:
Hal Leonard Australia Pty. Ltd.
4 Lentara Court
Cheltenham, Victoria, 3192 Australia
Email: info@halleonard.com.au

THE AVENGERS
from THE AVENGERS

TRUMPET

Composed by
ALAN SILVESTRI

© 2012 Marvel Superheroes Music
All Rights Reserved.   Used by Permission.

CAPTAIN AMERICA MARCH

from CAPTAIN AMERICA

TRUMPET

By ALAN SILVESTRI

© 2011 Marvel Comics Music
All Rights Reserved   Used by Permission

DOCTOR WHO XI

TRUMPET

By MURRAY GOLD

Copyright © 2010 BBC WORLDWIDE LTD. and UNIVERSAL MUSIC PUBLISHING LTD.
All Rights in the U.S. and Canada Administered by UNIVERSAL - POLYGRAM INTERNATIONAL PUBLISHING, INC.
All Rights Reserved   Used by Permission

DOWNTON ABBEY
(Theme)

TRUMPET

Music by JOHN LUNN

Copyright © 2010 DEPOTSOUND LTD. and DU VINAGE PUBLISHING
All Rights for DEPOTSOUND LTD. in the U.S. and Canada Controlled and Administered by
UNIVERSAL - POLYGRAM INTERNATIONAL PUBLISHING, INC.
All Rights for DU VINAGE PUBLISHING in the U.S. Administered by R3D MUSIC
All Rights Reserved   Used by Permission

GAME OF THRONES

Theme from the HBO Series GAME OF THRONES

TRUMPET

By RAMIN DJAWADI

Copyright © 2011 TL MUSIC PUBLISHING
All Rights Administered by UNIVERSAL MUSIC CORP.
All Rights Reserved   Used by Permission

GUARDIANS OF THE GALAXY

from GUARDIANS OF THE GALAXY

TRUMPET

Composed by TYLER BATES,
DIETER HARTMANN, TIMOTHY WILLIAMS
and KURT OLDMAN

© 2014 Marvel Superheroes Music and Marvel Comics Music
All Rights Reserved. Used by Permission.

HAWAII FIVE-O THEME

from the Television Series

TRUMPET

By MORT STEVENS

Copyright © 1969 Sony/ATV Music Publishing LLC and Aspenfair Music
Copyright Renewed
All Rights Administered by Sony/ATV Music Publishing LLC, 424 Church Street, Suite 1200, Nashville, TN 37219
International Copyright Secured   All Rights Reserved

MARRIED LIFE

from UP

TRUMPET

By MICHAEL GIACCHINO

© 2009 Walt Disney Music Company and Pixar Talking Pictures
All Rights Reserved.   Used by Permission.

OUTLANDER THEME
(The Skye Boat Song)

TRUMPET

Traditional Music
Arranged by BEAR McCREARY

Copyright © 2014 ole TV Avenue Music
All Rights Reserved   Used by Permission

PROLOGUE AND PROLOGUE PART 2

from BEAUTY AND THE BEAST

TRUMPET

PROLOGUE
Music by ALAN MENKEN

PROLOGUE PART 2
Music by ALAN MENKEN and CHRISTOPHER BENSTEAD

PROLOGUE
© 1991 Wonderland Music Company, Inc.
All Rights Reserved. Used by Permission.

PROLOGUE PART 2
© 2017 Wonderland Music Company, Inc. and Walt Disney Music Company
All Rights Reserved. Used by Permission.

REY'S THEME

from STAR WARS: THE FORCE AWAKENS

TRUMPET

Music by JOHN WILLIAMS

© 2015 Utapau Music
All Rights Reserved. Used by Permission.

THEME FROM THE X-FILES

from the Twentieth Century Fox Television Series THE X-FILES

TRUMPET

By MARK SNOW

Copyright © 1993, 1995 T C F Music Publishing, Inc.
All Rights Reserved   Used by Permission

TEST DRIVE

from the Motion Picture HOW TO TRAIN YOUR DRAGON

TRUMPET

By JOHN POWELL

Copyright © 2010 DWA SONGS
All Rights Administered by ALMO MUSIC CORP.
All Rights Reserved   Used by Permission